LORD'S

A Celebration in Pictures

LORD'S

A Celebration in Pictures

Andrew Strauss

PHILLIMORE

2014

Published by

PHILLIMORE BOOK PUBLISHING

ISBN 978-0-9927266-0-7

**Celebrating the
Bicentenary of Lord's**

Contents

Acknowledgements

Phillimore (Noel Osborne and Andrew Illes) and their project partners, Rick Mayston of Getty Images, and James Finlay, photographer, wish to thank members of the working party which has the responsibility for the arrangements to celebrate the Bicentenary in 2014 of the present Lord's Ground, and in particular Colin Maynard, Jon Robinson, Neil Robinson, Suzanne Robinson, Clare Causton and Clare Skinner for their invaluable expertise and cheerful guidance.

At Getty Images/Hulton Archive we have been greatly assisted by Matthew Butson, Damian Dent, Caroline Theakstone, and Sean Harry.

Lastly, we thank Andrew Strauss who has filled the dual role of author and picture selector with typical focus and flair.

Foreword
by H.R.H. The Duke of Edinburgh, K.G., K.T.
President of M.C.C., 1949 and 1974-75

BALMORAL CASTLE

I am quite sure that the publication of this book to mark the bicentenary of the present Lord's Ground will be warmly welcomed by cricket enthusiasts all over the world. Andrew Strauss deserves great credit as author and selector of the images to illustrate the development of what started as a rural cricket field into what is probably the most famous ground in the world.

Preface by J.M. Brearley, O.B.E. President of M.C.C., 2007-08

Lord's has been a microcosm of British, or perhaps English, society. It has had its snobberies. Lord Monkton, a member of several Conservative Cabinets during the 1950s, said once that "compared with the M.C.C. Committee, the Cabinet was a bunch of pinko's". Before the War, professionals playing in matches at Lord's would change in a basement room, with views of the cricket glimpsed through chairs and the legs of spectators seated in front of the Pavilion. I changed in this room as a schoolboy, going for nets with the old Middlesex coach, Jim Sims. It was here that I learned how to play shove ha'penny.

There is a story about an announcement made on the Ground in 1949. "Ladies and gentlemen, a correction to your scorecards: for F.J. Titmus read Titmus, F.J." This was on the first morning of Fred's first home match for Middlesex. His first away appearance had been at Bath, against Somerset, a week or two before, the first of my father's two appearances for Middlesex. Since Fred's last home match was also mine, in 1982, against Surrey, Fred would say, "I saw the father in, and the son out".

Yet despite its grandeur, as Andrew Strauss writes, the atmosphere of Lord's is "traditional but surprisingly unstuffy". It has always had the Tavern, which used to be situated just over the boundary at mid-wicket. I have a piece of its old mahogany bar as a table.

Lord's is noted for its slope. In the '50s and '60s its pitch also had a ridge; two ridges, in fact, but the bigger one was at the Nursery End. A fast bowler coming from the Pavilion End would get sometimes alarming bounce from the upslope of this ridge. In those days bowlers like Alan Moss, Fred Trueman, Brian Statham, Les Jackson and Jack Flavell were to be feared at Lord's.

The official line was "the ridge does not exist", but when the Ground flooded there was a lake through the middle of the pitch, with islands or hillocks at each end, just on a fast bowler's length. Which seemed to be fatal to the official view. I was reminded of the USA line, from *Beyond the Fringe* (1957) that "Red China does not exist". What we don't want to exist we make non-existent.

Lord's, through its owners, M.C.C., has moved gracefully with the times. The Ground has been developed and transformed, but not into a stadium. It has been one of the biggest achievements to have commissioned the work of excellent architects to create a whole with totally individual parts. We used to mock Gubby Allen's obsession with keeping the view of the trees behind the Nursery Ground; but now I'm completely at one with this requirement. It is part of Lord's' distinction that, for a major sporting ground (understated, as Strauss says), so close to the centre of a major city, it retains its link with rural England. It is not dwarfed by buildings, or by unsuitable massing.

Politically and socially, too, Lord's has moved with the times. Despite the cost of tickets, and the inevitable corporate associations, youngsters get in at very low ticket prices. In Test Match lunch intervals the outfield is full of children playing *kwik-cricket*; and there is an aura of friendliness and goodwill from those who work here. M.C.C. is increasingly aware of, and acts on, what it can offer to local communities.

Much thought and effort goes into the staging of every match played at the Ground. Each game has its own character and spirit, whether it is a Test Match or a Village Final. And visiting Test players, hardened Ashes warriors amongst them, are excited by its traditions. One said "And Bradman walked through here?!" Another was excited to be having lunch less than 50 yards from the Ashes Urn. Visiting Test players feel disappointed if their tour lacks a Test at Lord's.

I have been coming to Lord's since I was eight, brought first by my mother during the holidays, to watch Middlesex. I came to an Australia Test when I was eleven, and spent a shilling on a little book of Ashes scorecards. Later I was coached here, and played for M.C.C. schoolboys, and Middlesex Young Cricketers. I played in four Varsity matches at Lord's, and for many years for Middlesex. I was lucky enough to play also for England at Lord's. (Jim Sims' prediction – that he was sure I'd play for Middlesex, but not sure I'd play for England – was about right!) Latterly I have been on the Committee. I have loved the place for decades, and have now grown out of my awe – I once replied to a letter from Assistant Secretary Jim Dunbar, "Dear Lord Dunbar", maybe thinking he was a character in *Macbeth* – but with enhanced affection.

Introduction by Andrew Strauss, O.B.E.

Lord's Cricket Ground is quietly nestled amongst the high-rise apartment blocks of St John's Wood, a distinctly affluent and fashionable area of North West London. A plethora of residences has grown up around the venerable Ground, with inhabitants often paying a premium for the upper floors, and thus a view of the sacred turf. Even so, Lord's is an understated sporting presence. It does not dominate the landscape in the same way that Wembley Stadium or Twickenham overshadow their surrounding areas like great citadels of the ever-expanding sporting empire.

In fact, it is quite possible to walk along the perimeter walls of the Ground, but never to appreciate fully what goes on behind them. Lord's does not feel the need to show off her virtues. Once inside the Ground, however, the full majesty of the place begins to become apparent. This is a thoroughly modern cricketing facility, whose capacity of 28,500 makes it the largest of all the grounds in England. The contrast between new and old can be seen everywhere, but never is it more pronounced than the face-off between the immense presence of the Pavilion, which was built in 1889-90 by Thomas Verity, and the award-winning, nautically-inspired J.P. Morgan Media Centre, designed by the appropriately-named Future Systems and built in time for the 1999 Cricket World Cup.

What really impresses about the Ground, however, is not the architecture, although both the Grand Stand and the Mound Stand are among the best seating areas in the game of cricket. It is, instead, the aura of the place. The description that "Lord's is history modeled in turf and building" by J.M. Kilburn sums up, better than any other observation, the feeling one gets when setting foot on the Ground. Before your eyes lies the history of the game of cricket. Its laws, its governance, its evolution, and its place in society today are on display, without any need to visit the excellent Museum, which hides behind the Pavilion. The Ground, itself, is a museum.

The man whose name the Ground bears, Thomas Lord, himself a professional cricketer from northern farming stock, managed to get funding from some wealthy benefactors to start a new private cricket ground in 1787. The site, in Dorset Square, rapidly became too expensive to run, and in 1811 he moved away from the hustle and bustle of central London to the far more genteel setting of St John's Wood. The location he chose lay barely a mile from the present site, but when the land was requisitioned by the government in order to build the Regent's Canal, a further move was necessitated, this time to the present location. Lord's Cricket Ground opened for business on 22nd June 1814, with a match between M.C.C. and Hertfordshire.

The Ground, in its early days, looked far more like the type of quaint cricketing setting found in an isolated village in the countryside than the international venue it is today. It was even accompanied by a series of ponds, where the Mound Stand now sits, to complete the rural setting. The original Pavilion, about which very little information remains, was essentially a wooden hut, and the contrast between it and its second replacement, the current Pavilion, could not be greater. The first Pavilion burnt down in 1825, and was replaced by a larger structure, which evolved alongside the rest of the Ground before finally being replaced by the current Pavilion in time for the 1890 season. By then, the Ground was firmly established as the most important in the land, complete with stands for spectators, parking for horse-drawn carriages beside the playing area, and the various dining and leisure facilities we have come to expect from Test Match grounds.

Perhaps it goes without saying that Lord's is the home of M.C.C., so closely are the two intertwined. Marylebone Cricket Club, founded in 1787, quickly became the ultimate authority on all things cricket. The Club published its first version of the laws of the game in 1788, and for almost 200 years M.C.C. ran and oversaw all cricket around the world. Lord's was the epicentre of cricketing power and influence. Although many of M.C.C.'s powers have been ceded to other bodies in recent years, the governorship of the Laws of Cricket continues, alongside a healthy and vibrant membership of over 18,000 people. Membership waiting lists remain stubbornly around the twenty-year mark. The privileges accorded to those Members include use of the Real Tennis court, squash courts and indoor cricket facilities, but primarily entry to and use of the Pavilion during cricket.

As a player, I found the most striking time to see Lord's was on the first morning of an important Test Match.

It is at this time when the Ground, which can lie dormant for months on end in the winter, is teeming with life. Approaching along St John's Wood Road, heading for the players' parking facilities, it was almost impossible to miss the never-ending queues, stretching for well over a mile, full of M.C.C. Members anxiously waiting for the opening of the gates at the stroke of 9 a.m. There is no reserved seating in the Pavilion, and the plummest seating positions, either in the Long Room or behind the bowler's arm, are secured only with the considerable effort of arriving at the Ground at 5 a.m. and waiting at the front of the queue. Those who arrive later must wait patiently for their turn, and will have to fight over the proverbial scraps left behind by those preceding them.

The low buzz of anticipation that accompanies those who are queuing, discussing the day's prospects and the like, was always likely to set off the first of many surges of adrenalin racing through my veins. Once safely within the confines of the Ground itself, the players' route to the Pavilion takes them past the M.C.C. Museum. It is a treasure trove of cricketing artefacts, relics and mementoes, many loaned or donated by former or current players. Its most famous treasure is, of course, the Ashes Urn, which, although impossibly small and fragile, holds almost as much history and tradition alongside its ashen entrails as the whole of Lord's Cricket Ground. I am still taken aback every time I see the Urn in the flesh.

Given that the future, and not the past, is on the player's mind, he is unlikely to choose the hours before the start of a Test Match to meander around the Museum. Instead, he will walk through the Pavilion door, be greeted by the incredibly friendly and polite Pavilion stewards, before making his way through the Long Room en route to the Dressing Room.

The players' changing facility is Lord's Cricket Ground in a microcosm. It is a large space, but not so large as to feel cavernous. It has all the mod cons, flat-screen TVs and the like, but is still able to feel traditional. The Honours Boards in particular, filled with the names of cricketers through the ages who have managed to score centuries or take five wickets, provide a poignant link with the past. Moreover, it is warm and welcoming, although perhaps much of the atmosphere of the room is provided by the dressing room attendants, who are unparalleled throughout the world in the quality of their service.

Cameron and Pete are able to provide anything a player might possibly desire: food, magazines, studs for boots, cigarettes – all are readily available. More exotic items might have to be sourced, but they will be found.

No pre-match routine will ever be complete without a stroll across the main playing area, under the J.P. Morgan Media Centre, to the secondary playing facility, the Nursery Ground, where the practice nets are housed. Unsurprisingly, the Nursery Ground is so named because it was once Henderson's Nursery, growing pineapples and tulips, before being purchased by the Club in 1887. Some minor matches are played on its surface, but during all Test and First-Class matches, it is reserved entirely for practice. Rows of beautifully manicured practice pitches are available, as well as several areas set aside for various fielding drills. To have a practice area of that size in London of all places is quite extraordinary. Having played for both Middlesex and England at Lord's for over fifteen years, I have seen every inch of those practice facilities, often spending entire days trying to come to terms with one technical deficiency or another.

Many of the more advanced technical aids, ranging from bowling machines to speed guns and video equipment, are housed in the Cricket Academy, which was rebuilt in 1995, complete with opening sides to let in natural light. There is also a gym, a bar and a viewing gallery for coaches and parents alike to watch aspiring cricketers being put through their paces during the winter courses.

If the weather is fine, it is unlikely that many Test players will be found indoors during the final preparations for a game. The Cricket Academy comes into its own when inclement English weather interrupts proceedings. Traditionally, Lord's has suffered tremendously from the weather. The outfield, which was originally transported by Mr Lord from ground to ground, had been particularly prone to flooding and saturation, spelling the premature end of many a promising day of cricket. It was re-laid in 2003, when the clay-based top soil was replaced with a much faster drying and better draining sand-based version. The speed at which the new outfield dries has caused more than one player to be found wanting after "pushing the gamble button", and venturing into the nightspots of London, while the rain poured down the evening before play. I was certainly amazed that the second day of the Test Match against India in 2007 started so shortly after one of the heaviest deluges I can remember left much of the lower part of the outfield completely submerged. The new outfield has proved a sound investment by the Club.

While the players are busy preparing themselves, the spectators are pouring through the gates, eager for the start of the game. The Pavilion apart, where only jackets and ties, or long skirts and covered shoulders for the ladies, are permitted, the dress code at Lord's is nowadays mainly casual. The days when top hats and tails were commonplace are long gone. Lord's is traditional but surprisingly unstuffy away from the inner sanctum of the Pavilion.

It is still, though, a place to be seen. Often cricket-loving celebrities, from Stephen Fry to Mick Jagger – both Members of the Club – can be found surveying the scene from one of the corporate boxes, and it would not be surprising to find a former Prime Minister or two enjoying the pastime. Sir John Major often feeds his passion for the game at Lord's, and Sir Alec Douglas-Home, the only Prime Minister to have played first-class cricket, was another regular supporter.

In fact, politics and Lord's Cricket Ground have met many times before. During both the World Wars of the last century, the Ground was used by the Armed Forces. Between 1914 and 1918 soldiers were trained in wireless, military cooking and artillery at the Ground, to me a somewhat strange combination, but no doubt full of sense at the time. It was used by the RAF in the Second World War, but cricket did still take place occasionally, including while Hitler's V2 rockets were landing and exploding uncomfortably nearby. It goes without saying that many good cricketers and Members were lost in those conflicts.

Perhaps the most famous contretemps between Lord's and politics came with the initial non-selection, and the subsequent about-turn, of Basil D'Oliveira to tour South Africa with M.C.C. in 1968. It was a decision reached in the Lord's Committee Room, which set in place a series of events that strained to breaking point the relationship between Britain and South Africa. Eventually the South African government's refusal to let the tour proceed signalled the beginning of the end for South African international cricket under Apartheid, and the subsequent demonstrations prior to South Africa's proposed return

tour in 1970 left Lord's looking like a battlefield in its own right.

The Ground will never, in all likelihood, be able to shake off entirely the cloak of politics, either of an international or cricketing nature. The offices of the England and Wales Cricket Board lie within the premises, and M.C.C. is still an influential voice in world cricket, albeit a quieter one in this age. As John Arlott remarked, however, "Say that cricket has nothing to do with politics, and you say that cricket has nothing to do with life."

As the spectators start making their way to their allocated seats, the players will be back in the refuge of their respective dressing rooms, going through their various last-minute rituals in order to quell the nerves and prepare the body. These last agonising minutes before going out to bat were always the most challenging for me as an opening batsman. There is too much suppressed energy, anticipation and impatience to contend with. Spending a few moments on the surprisingly small players' balcony in order to adjust my eyes to the light was an integral part of my coping mechanism. Surveying the Ground in all its glory, complete with a full house of highly expectant fans, served to remind me just how fortunate I was to be representing my country in this magnificent amphitheatre.

The most iconic view of Lord's is that of the Pavilion, steadfastly guarded at the edge of the playing area by the Warner and Allen Stands, to its left and right respectively. However, it says a huge amount for the architecture of the Ground that my favourite view was looking out from the dressing room balcony towards the J.P. Morgan Media Centre, itself nestled between the Compton and Edrich Stands, and through to the Nursery Ground behind. The view of the trees behind the Nursery Ground, always a favourite of Members, as well as the distinct character of the various stands, pointedly reminds everyone that this is not a stadium; it is a cricket ground. It is relatively simple to build a circular concrete structure to house people; it is far more difficult to create a combination of buildings that define a history of a sport. That is what has been created at Lord's.

Adjoining the north end of the Pavilion is an extension that houses the Bowlers' Bar. Prior to satisfying the alcoholic requirements of Members, the room was used as the dressing room of the professional cricketers. In line with tradition, they were only deemed worthy enough to share a dressing room with their amateur team mates in 1946. On a balcony outside the bar hangs a large bell. This bell, dubbed "the worker" by the players, signals that play is about to get under way, and is rung five minutes before the start of every day's play and during Test Matches by a cricketing dignitary. For me, this sound generally brought relief. No more wondering what may be in store; it was time for action.

The route for a batsman from the dressing room to the playing area is a somewhat complicated one for the uninitiated. The slightly hazardous trip down the flight of stairs is made more difficult as the player has to pass hoards of Members making their way, in the opposite direction, towards their seats. Even protected by pads and helmet, swimming against this tide can be a difficult task to complete, and is potentially disorientating. It may go some way to explaining why David Steele, in his first Test Match at the Ground, continued down the next set of stairs into the basement of the building, rather than making his way towards the Long Room. Mishaps of that nature rarely bode well for a successful day at the crease.

For those who are able to navigate along the correct path, the Long Room now awaits. From there it is a short walk of no more than twenty-five yards to the door exiting the Pavilion and leading to the outfield. There is no more celebrated a walk in world cricket. During a Test Match the room is absolutely packed with Members, all hurriedly parted by the stewards to create a path for the players to make their way through to the Ground. To walk through the room, with Members barely a yard away from you on each side, all cheering in unison, is a particularly emotional experience. At a time when cold, logical heads are needed in order to negotiate the new ball, the heart is beating like a drum, and the hairs on the back of your neck are standing on end. Nowhere in world cricket allows players to be so closely intertwined with spectators prior to performing. I never came nearly as close as losing my composure under the weight of public support and anticipation as when Marcus Trescothick and I made our way through the Long Room to face the Australians at the start of the 2005 Test. Tears of pride were simmering below the surface.

Unfortunately, what the Long Room gives, it can take away. Barely 20 minutes after that rapturous applause, I again faced the journey through the Long Room, this time on my way back to the dressing room, having been caught off the bowling of Glenn McGrath for only 2 runs. The stony-faced silence that greeted my return could not have been a greater contrast to the outward journey. Hopes and dreams were in the midst of being shattered, and Members were in no mood for charity.

Arrival on the outfield itself is made by passing through a gate separating the uncovered Members' seating at the front of the Pavilion and the playing surface. Once through that gate, the angle of the slope of the Ground, running from the high point, at the northern end of the Ground, in front of the Grand Stand down towards the Mound and Tavern Stands sitting at the opposite end, becomes apparent. It has been measured as 6 feet 6 inches, but it feels much more than that. From a cricketer's point of view, it is the major quirk of the Ground. Inexperienced bowlers find it hard to maintain the correct line, whereas batsmen face an endless struggle to keep balance and to judge which balls to play and which to leave. Even on the most placid of wickets, it keeps players from both sides on their respective toes.

When the wicket was first constructed, all those years ago, it was famed for its dangerous and unpredictable nature. Some first-class counties refused to play at the Ground out of fear for their physical well-being, but in recent years it has tended to favour batsmen. I certainly found the wicket a pleasure to bat on, unless there was humidity in the air, which brought with it prodigious swing. Spinners in recent times have found the going particularly tough.

No one will ever know the intricacies of negotiating the Lord's wicket better than W. G. Grace. He is, without doubt, M.C.C.'s most famous Playing Member. Of his 870 first-class matches, 205 were played on the Ground, and he scored 28 centuries. Across 44 seasons he carried the game of cricket forward, becoming its face, and profiting handsomely from his fame. The cast-iron Members' main gates to the Ground, situated on St John's Wood Road, are named in his honour, and, nearly one hundred years after his death, his name, and stature as one of cricket's greatest players, still lives on.

For any player lucky enough to be representing his country at Lord's, the ambition of scoring a century or taking five or more wickets burns more brightly than at other grounds. It is partly about getting your name on the Honours Boards, but still more about being able to raise both arms to acknowledge the applause of a full house, knowing that you have done it on the grandest stage of all. For me, jumping this hurdle at the first attempt, on my debut in 2004 against New Zealand, will forever be one of the true highlights of my career. It was the fulfilment of a dream that had stayed with me from childhood, through my apprenticeship at Middlesex, and had accompanied me out to bat on that fateful day. There simply is no better feeling in cricket.

Somewhat surprisingly, many of the modern-day greats of the game have come to Lord's, seen Lord's, but have failed to conquer her. Sachin Tendulkar, Brian Lara, Ricky Ponting, Jacques Kallis and Shane Warne have all failed to get their names immortalised on the Honours Boards in the visitors' dressing rooms. I have no doubt that they all felt an increased pressure every time they played at the Home of Cricket. Being tourists, their chances have been few and far between, but striving to fulfill a destiny makes the game far more complicated.

Fittingly, the greatest player of them all, Don Bradman, did not suffer the same affliction. He scored two centuries at the Ground, holding the record for the highest score by a visiting player of 254, until an impetuous 23-year-old South African called Graeme Smith had the nerve to replace him at the top of the list.

If there has been one player of the modern era who has dominated the Ground more than any other, it would have to be Graham Gooch. I remember my first visit to the Ground as a young teenager in 1990, watching the opening day of the England v India Test Match. Gooch finished the day 194 not out en route to compiling 333, the highest score on the Ground. He followed it up with 123 in the second innings, and went on to score more than 2,000 Test runs at Lord's alone. As I made my way home that day, I had seen Test Match cricket in all its glory for the first time, and I had also found my first cricketing hero.

To me, though, cricket at Lord's is not about individual milestones. It is more about showcasing the game of cricket, and all it has to offer. Test Matches have always been the jewel in the crown of the Ground. However, a staple diet of first-class cricket, One Day Internationals, and most recently Twenty20 cricket have kept the

groundstaff busy from April to September. Schoolboys' matches, in the guise of Eton against Harrow, as well as the traditional clash between Oxford and Cambridge, are still played at the Ground. In addition, the increasingly popular and tremendously successful England Women's Team has had the opportunity to play here regularly.

In accordance with the moving times, permanent floodlights were erected in 2007 to ensure that the Ground was not left behind by other progressive county committees, and perhaps most surprisingly other sports, in the form of hockey, lacrosse, and most recently archery, have been given permission to use the facilities. It is fair to say that the use of Lord's for the Olympics in 2012 provided some of the Games' most stand-out spectacles.

Despite the hyperbole surrounding the "Mecca" of cricket, those that play and work at the Ground see it in a more personal light. For every day that the Ground delights spectators, Members and players alike by hosting games of cricket, there are far more when the great stands are empty, and cricket is not in progress. It is at these times that perhaps you get closer to the soul of the place.

M.C.C. employs nearly two hundred people, who scurry around the Ground in a host of different guises. There is always maintenance going on, from gardening to painting, with great care and attention paid to keeping the Ground in pristine condition. M.C.C.'s offices are situated both in the Pavilion, and behind it in the building that houses the Real Tennis and squash courts. Tours, membership and the day-to-day running of the Club are administered by the staff, headed by the Chief Executive and Secretary, Derek Brewer.

The Middlesex office is also situated in a building to the back of the Pavilion, and although Middlesex has been a tenant at the Ground since 1877, the relationship between the county and M.C.C. has never been better. Despite not owning their own ground, all at Middlesex are entitled to feel very fortunate to treat Lord's as their office.

The catering staff are always around, preparing for one of the many functions that take place on non-match days. Lord's has to earn her keep. They are also responsible for the sumptuous feasts that are enjoyed by the players on every day of a match. Sports nutrition has come a long way in recent years, but the players are all thankful that it has failed to find its way through the Grace Gates. Rib-eye steaks, bowls of chips and sticky toffee puddings still rule the roost in the Lord's Pavilion kitchens.

Finally, there are the custodians of the Ground: the stewards, who are able to maintain a jovial, good natured presence, but are not inclined to suffer fools gladly. They add tremendously to the atmosphere of the place.

What all these people have in common is a deep-rooted and long-standing affection for the place. Lord's may be capable of dazzling newcomers when fully laden with crowd and atmosphere in the middle of an Australian Test Match, but to me it is significant that her charms still rub off on those that see her every day. In fact, it is apt that Lord's Cricket Ground mirrors the game of cricket so symmetrically. She can entertain people with her charms and facilities, much like a Twenty20 or One Day game. However, Test cricket is a game that cannot be fully appreciated without time. The nuances and subtle plots of the game reveal themselves only if the viewer is willing to invest in the pursuit. Similarly, to appreciate fully the great value and presence of Lord's, you need to devote some time and effort to the task. By doing this, you will be able to uncover the multitude of minute detail that has served to make the Ground the "Home of Cricket" for 200 years.

LORD'S

A Celebration in Pictures

Two Sonnets by G.H.G. Doggart, O.B.E.
President of M.C.C., 1981-82

The years, 1814 and 1815, saw two events crucial to anyone reading this. Each event is associated with one key figure. The juxtaposition of the two events (surely already identified by most) – the victory of the Duke of Wellington at Waterloo in 1815, "by a whisker" and not without Prussian help; and, in 1814, the continuing faith of Thomas Lord in moving his precious turf for the third time – suggested to me a Sonnet about each.

In "Lord's, 1814" and "Waterloo, 1815" – ideally, perhaps, read in reverse chronological order – an eye-witness from the Parish of Marylebone and a survivor from the battle of Waterloo reflect on what one had observed and the other experienced. Both clearly attached radical importance to what they later recall.

May Thomas Lord, Lord's Ground and those who serve it, and, not least because of our Parish Church nearby, the Lord himself be justly praised in 2014.

Lord's, 1814

An Eye-Witness Reflects in the Year of W.G. Grace's Birth, 1848

The Eyre estate was crucial. I was there
When Thomas Lord – once servant and net-bowler
Of the White Conduit Club removed his roller,
His horse, and much-loved turf, from Dorset Square.
I saw him also move again the core
Of his bequest to Cricket's future strength
When "that Canal" – precisely "on a length"?! –
Was swept across his second ground – by law.
The third Lord's ground from 1814 flourished,
With wise decisions from the M.C.C.,
Not least persuading Ward the ground be nourished –
Yes, he who holds the record score in fee.
My high-held hopes were clear: A first-class "wicket";
And Lord's being called, world-wide, "The Home of Cricket".

Waterloo, 1815

A Combatant Remembers in the Year that William Ward
made 278 for M.C.C. v. Norfolk, 1820

I was at Hougoumont when the French attacked,
And we were told the battle would be lost,
Or won, by how we fought, and what the cost
Would clearly be if our formation cracked.
Later, one question centred on just who
Deserved the credit – Wellington or Blücher?
Our only thought? Would victory bring us lucre
Now that the French had met their Waterloo?
In retrospect, I've come to realise
How critical it was that our line held,
Those hours at Hougoumont under fire-red skies,
By British bloody-mindedness impelled.
"We Few" left murmur, as we drink our ale,
Thank God that we were there – and did not fail.

Thomas Lord

Born in Thirsk, Yorkshire, in 1755, Lord was a professional cricketer who played as a ground-staff bowler from 1787 to 1802, and was mostly associated with Middlesex County Cricket Club and M.C.C. His first recorded match was for Middlesex against Essex in 1787, on his, the original Lord's Ground – a seven-acre plot off Dorset Square which he acquired for the White Conduit Club, soon to merge into Marylebone Cricket Club.

The lease on the original Ground ran out in 1810, and he obtained an 80-year lease on Brick Field and Great Field at North Bank, St John's Wood. This second venue was built in 1809 and M.C.C. relocated there in 1811. However, it was not to last: two years later Parliament requisitioned the Ground for the Regent's Canal, so Lord moved again, literally taking his turf with him.

The present Ground opened in 1814, but Lord soon found that he was not making enough money, so he obtained permission to develop part of the Ground for housing, leaving only some 150 square yards for the playing area. This was not a popular proposal and, to counter it, William Ward, a noted batsman and director of the Bank of England, bought out Lord for £5,000. Despite this change of ownership, the Ground continues to this day to bear Lord's name.

Lord left St John's Wood in 1830 and retired to West Meon in Hampshire, not far from Hambledon. He died in 1832 and is buried in the churchyard of St John's Church.

The year 1955 was the bicentenary of Lord's birth. To mark it, Lord's presented the cricketers of Thirsk with an oak plaque. At West Meon an M.C.C. team walked with local cricketers from the pavilion to the churchyard to pay respects to Thomas Lord at his tomb.

1 Thomas Lord's tombstone in the churchyard of West Meon, Hampshire.

LORD'S CRICKET GROUND
CENTENARY

1814   1851   1885

1814   1914

1914

TOM BROWNE & Co (NOTT'S) LIMITED.

LORD'S GROUND.

M.C.C. v. HERTFORDSHIRE,
JUNE 22nd, 1814.

1st Innings. HERTFORDSHIRE.		2nd Innings.	
Mowbray, c Ward	4	b Beauclerk	1
H. Bentley, not out	33	run out	0
Bruton, b Budd	7	b Osbaldeston	17
S. Carter, b Budd	0	st Vigne	0
Sibley, b Beauclerk	6	c Budd	1
Taylor, c Beauclerk	6	run out	2
Denham, b Budd	10	st Vigne	21
T. Carter, b Budd	1	b Osbaldeston	0
J. Sibley, c Beauclerk	6	not out	3
Freeman, c Beauclerk	2	run out	5
Crew, b Beauclerk	0	st Vigne	0
Byes	4	Byes	5
Total	79	Total	55

M.C.C.

Mr. A. Schabner, c J. Sibley	55
Hon. D. Kinnaird, b S. Carter	1
Mr. C. Warren, b Taylor	25
Mr. E. H. Budd, c T. Carter	36
Hon. E. Bligh, b Bentley	6
Mr. T. Burgoyne, run out	0
Lord F. Beauclerk, b Taylor	3
Mr. G. Osbaldeston, b Mowbray	18
Mr. W. Ward, run out	10
Mr. T. Vigne, b Bentley	2
Mr. J. Poulet, not out	1
Byes	4
Total	161

2   The match between M.C.C. and Hertfordshire on 22nd June 1814 was the first to be played at Thomas Lord's new ground. It went ahead despite the fact that, just four days earlier, "the public house there was rocked by a great explosion in which the landlady, her sister and four girls were seriously burnt. The two former in a dangerous way."

The teams were headed by Lord Frederick Beauclerk, great-grandson of Charles II and Nell Gwyn, an amateur and probably the finest player of his era, and "Squire" Osbaldeston, a famous all-round sportsman: rider to hounds, fisherman, shot, fighter and gambler.

3 Poster for a Grand Match at Lord's New Cricket Ground, 6th June 1816 and the following day between two Select Elevens of All England.

4   Cricket at Lord's in 1822. A watercolour attributed to George Cruickshank.

5   The Corinthians at Lord's in 1822.

6   In 1825, William Ward rescued part of the Ground from the developers, when Lord proposed to build seven pairs of houses on the Ground, leaving a mere 150 square yards for cricket. Ward took over the lease for £5,400. He was a director of the Bank of England and became MP for the City of London.

He had become famous for scoring the highest individual innings then made at Lord's: 278 for M.C.C. against Norfolk.

In the early hours of 29th July 1825, just after Ward had extended and decorated it, the Lord's pavilion was burnt to the ground, and all the records of M.C.C. and its trophies were destroyed.

7   John Nyren's *Young Cricketer's Tutor*, published in 1833: frontispiece showing Lord's Cricket Ground.

8 Lord's in a print by G.H. Laporte, *c.*1835.

9 J.H. Dark, portrait by J.C. Anderson. In 1836 Dark took over the lease of Lord's for £2,000 and an annuity of £425. He is listed in the 1851 census as "proprietor of houses". Lord's had post-and-chain fencing and a patch in the middle of the bumpy grass was constantly rolled for the cricket. It was a generally ridge-and-furrow surface. The pitch itself was uneven and often stony. Scythes were not allowed, mowers not yet invented. Creases on the pitch were cut with a knife. Lord's at this time was described by batsmen as "bumpy and dangerous" and by bowlers as "full of life and spirit".

As Tony Lewis comments, "The grass was kept low by sheep which were penned up on match days. As many as 400 sheep would be driven on to the pitch some Saturdays to chew around before being ushered to Smithfield Market on Monday. They cleaned the herbage and then the boys went round after them to pick up the rough stalks." (See no.12)

10   The 50th anniversary of the Marylebone Club was celebrated in the "Grand Jubilee Match" played between the North and South of England on 10th and 11th July 1837.

11   The match in progress between the North and South of England, 10 July 1837, which was attended by 3,000 spectators on both days. After two days of excellent cricket the South beat the North, thanks in no small part to Lillywhite's 14 wickets, even though they had given their opponents Box, the Sussex stumper, and Cobbett, the Surrey spinner.

12 Lord's Cricket Ground, 1837.

13 In 1837 J.H. Dark built a running track, which consisted of a path around the field, 7ft 6ins wide and 640ft long. Here, from the *London Illustrated News*, is a foot hurdle-race at Lord's in 1842.

14 The Scorer, William Davies, painted by T. Hayward in 1842.

15 & 16 Dark also met commercial success, when he encouraged businessmen to hire marquees and display their wares at the encampment of the Ioway Indians in August 1844.

17 Lord's on a Grand Match Day in 1851; an engraving after J.C. Anderson.

18 J.H. Dark personally paid for the draining of the playing area. "Four hundred loads of clay were taken out, and the same quantity of gravel laid on the pipes" at a cost of £300, according to the 1850 *Lillywhite's Guide*. However, Lord's was a terrible playing surface, and on match days searching for a decent pitch was a continuing problem when the one prepared might have a deep hole in it.

CRICKETING.
(Lord Cricket Ground, St John's Wood, Match of the Gentlemen & Players.)
Drawn expressly for the "Book of Field Sports."

London: Henry Lea, 22, Warwick Lane.

19   R.A. FitzGerald took over as the first paid Secretary in 1863, and one of his first tasks was to improve the Lord's pitch: the surface was still rough and uneven. This lithograph, drawn especially for the *Book of Field Sports*, illustrates a Gentlemen v Players match in *c.*1864. The levelling was not finished until 1875, by which time there had been a tragedy. In 1870 the Nottinghamshire cricketer George Summers was hit on the head by a ball while at the crease. The ball perhaps pitched on a stone. Summers returned to his father's house in Nottingham for treatment, and died there four days after the match finished.

20 The Pavilion, 1865-89, by Frank Verity. Under R.A. FitzGerald's supervision, the Pavilion was expanded to include two additional wings, a room for players in the basement, and accommodation for Members and guests on a flat roof. There was a new façade, a Committee room, a library and a new dressing room.

21 The Australian Cricketers, 1882.

Back row (left to right): H.H. Massie, G.J. Bonner,
S.P. Jones, F.R. Spofforth.

Middle row: C.W. Beal, J.M. Blackham, G. Giffen,
W.L. Murdoch, A.C. Bannerman, P.S. McDonnell,
H.F. Boyle.

Front row: G.E. Palmer, W.T. Garrett.

22   Lord's Cricket Ground, 19th-century panorama. In 1878, Peter Pearce, the groundsman,
described Lord's as "so smooth, so firm, so well covered with herbage". However, after a wet
summer and heavy rains, the result was "... mucky, messy, muddy wickets".

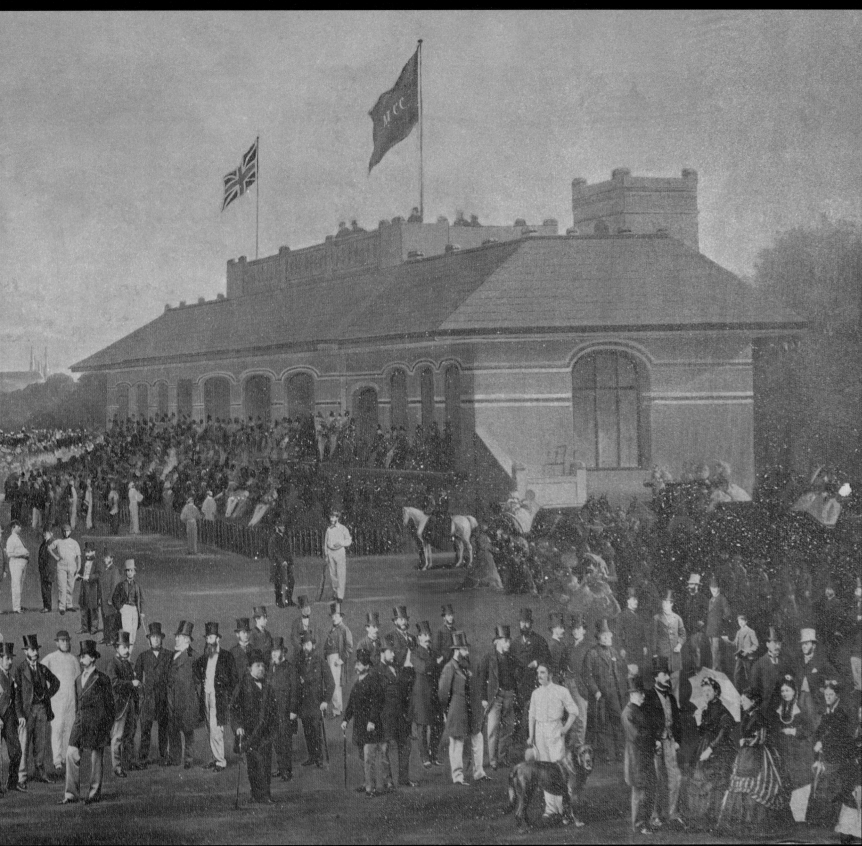

OXFORD v CAMBRIDGE
1885
by H.W. Marshall, R.W.S.

23 Oxford v Cambridge at Lord's in 1885, a watercolour by H.W. Marshall, R.W.S. This fixture dates back to 1827 when the first match was played between the two universities at Lord's.

24 Eton v Harrow, 1886, by Albert Chevallier Tayler. Eton's inaugural match against Harrow at Lord's was played at the first ground in 1805. It was also notable as Lord Byron was in the Harrow team. The first match at this ground between the two schools took place in 1818, when Eton won by an innings and two runs.

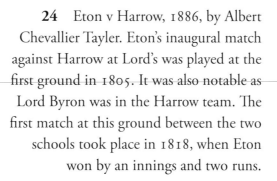

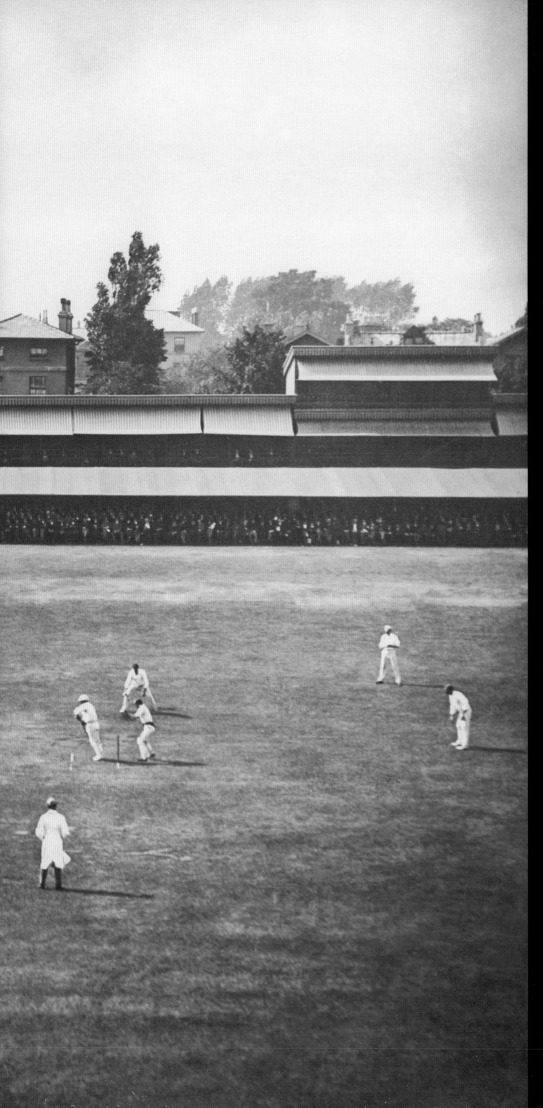

25 The year 1887 marked the centenary of the Marylebone Club. This image, showing the original Grand Stand, is of the match played between Gentlemen and Players on 11th July 1887, a year in which Queen Victoria's Golden Jubilee was also celebrated.

Also, in the centenary year, Henderson's Nursery, or the Pine Apples as it was often called, was acquired by M.C.C., adding a further 3½ acres to Lord's Ground. It was fitting that the Nursery End would now provide for practice and the nurturing of cricketers; formerly practice nets were on the outfield.

26 This painting by H. Barrable and R. Ponsonby Staples, conjures up an imaginary scene in M.C.C.'s centenary year, 1887. The Prince and Princess of Wales (later King Edward VII and Queen Alexandra) approach seats in "A" Stand (from 1958 the Warner Stand), where Lillie Langtry the actress is sitting to the right of the stanchion. In the match, W.G. Grace is batting, F.R. Spofforth bowling, and bending to the ball is T.W. Garrett.

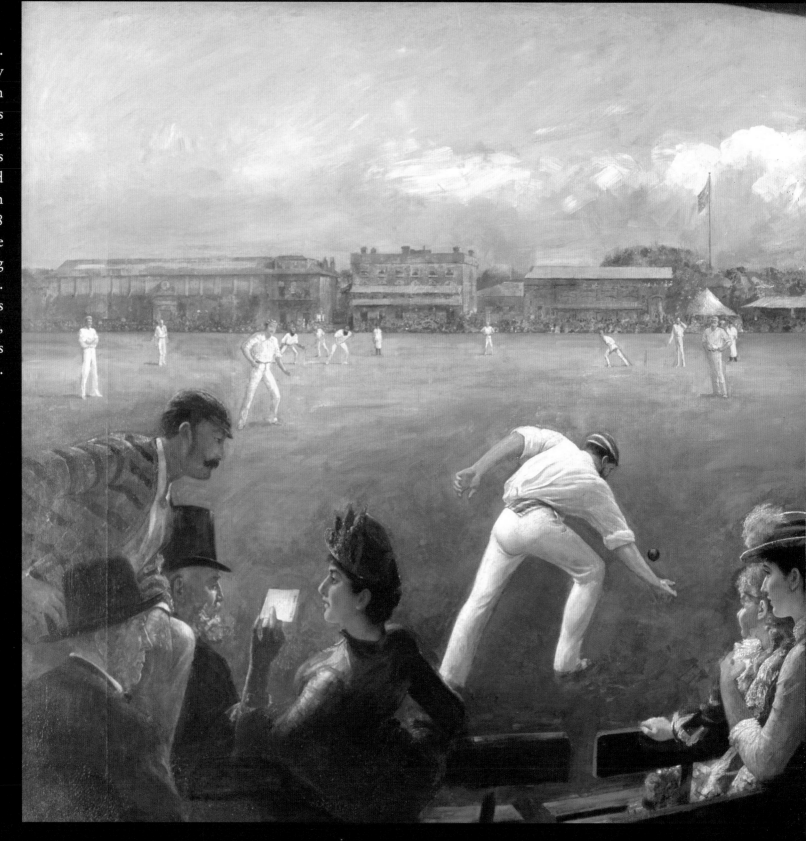

· R.G. BARLOW · · W. SCOTTON · · W. BARNES · · A.N. HORNBY · · Hon. A. LYTTELTON · · W.G. GRACE · · A.G. STEEL · · LORD HARRIS · · G. ULYETT · · W.W. READ · · A. SHREWSBURY ·

T.W. GARRETT · P.S. McDONNELL · S.P. JONES · A.C. BANNERMAN · H.J.H. SCOTT · F.R. SPOFFORTH · G. GIFFEN · G.E. PALMER · J. McC. BLACKHAM · W.L. MURDOCH · G.J. BONNOR

27   Eton v. Harrow match, luncheon interval, *c.*1890.

28 "Lord's in Danger: M.C.C. go out to meet the Enemy." Cartoon based on the text, "Sir Edward Watkin proposes to construct a Railway passing through Lord's Cricket Ground". In 1891 by Act of Parliament the Manchester, Sheffield & Lincolnshire Railway later the Great Central Railway were authorised to build tunnels from Marylebone Station running under the eastern fringe of Lord's Cricket Ground. This proposal had been strongly opposed by M.C.C., but finally the matter was settled by the Club giving up part of the freehold of the Practice Ground in exchange for a larger area occupied by the Clergy Female Orphanage School on the condition that M.C.C. was granted a 99-year lease of the ground immediately over the tunnels. *c.*1891.

29 M.C.C. was given by the Great Central Railway, in exchange for permission to tunnel under the Practice Ground, the site of the Clergy Female Orphanage School on the corner of St John's Wood Road and Wellington Road. A former pupil is quoted: "How envious we were of those few girls who were allowed to go on the roof of the house with the mistresses to watch a cricket match at Lord's …" 1891.

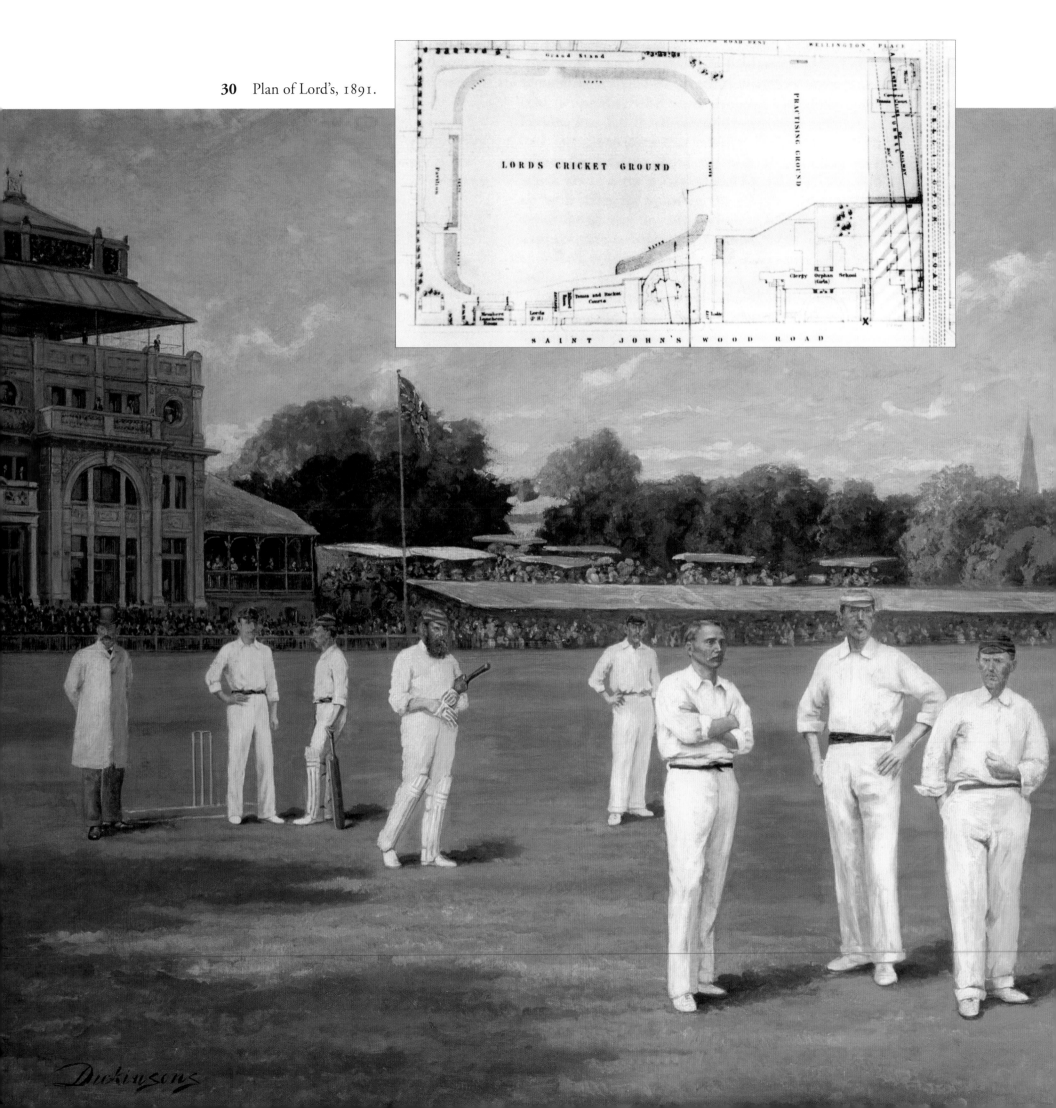

30 Plan of Lord's, 1891.

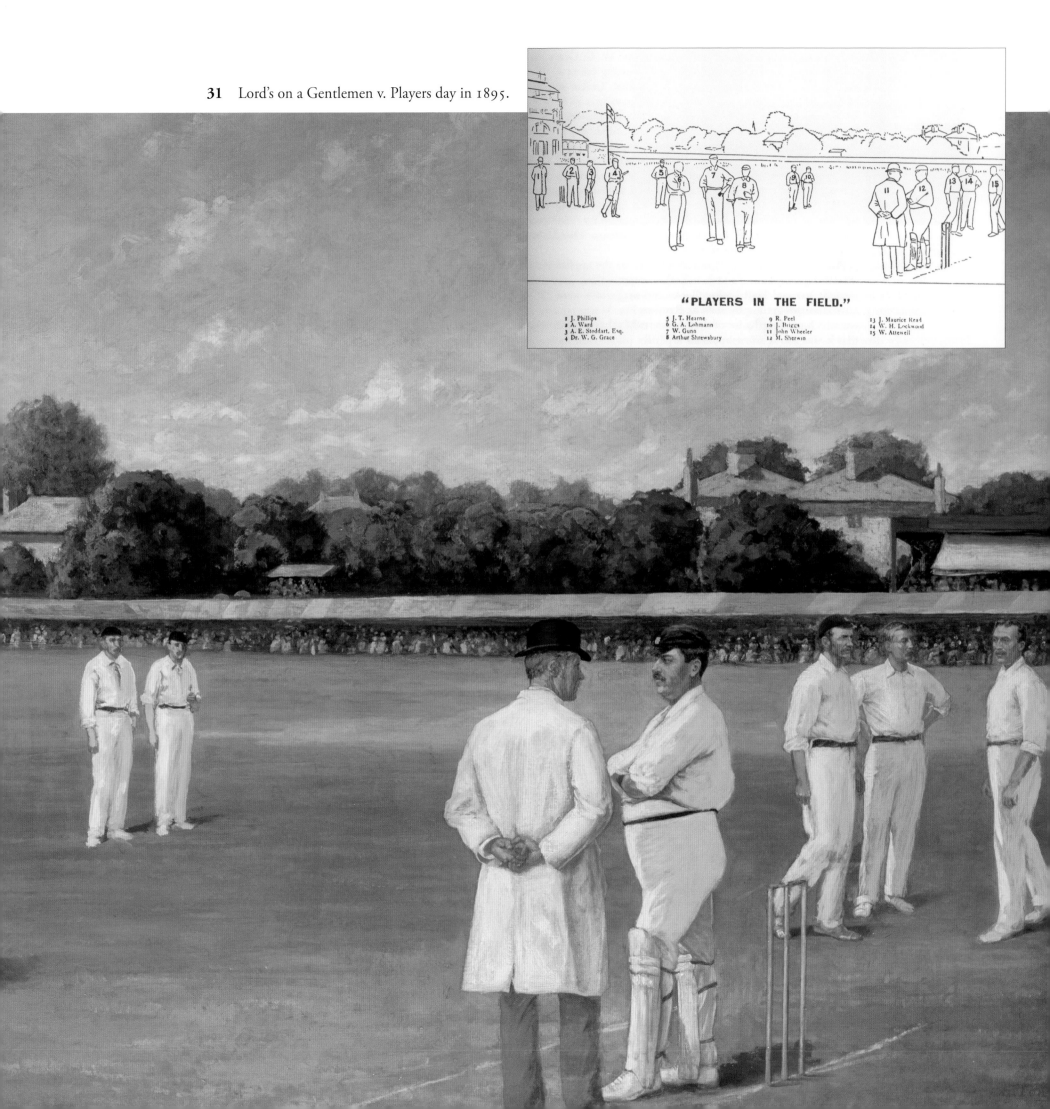

"PLAYERS IN THE FIELD."

1 J. Phillips	5 J. T. Hearne	9 R. Peel	13 J. Maurice Read
2 A. Ward	6 G. A. Lohmann	10 J. Briggs	14 W. H. Lockwood
3 A. E. Stoddart, Esq.	7 W. Gunn	11 John Wheeler	15 W. Attewell
4 Dr. W. G. Grace	8 Arthur Shrewsbury	12 M. Sherwin	

32 Tunnelling work at Lord's in December 1896.

33   Painting of Dr W.G. Grace of Gloucestershire and England, batting at Lord's, *c.*1895.

Much has been written about W.G. Grace's prowess as a cricketer. He himself reckoned his finest innings to have been for the Gentlemen against the Players in 1868, when he scored 134, all run, on a dreadful pitch at Lord's, out of the Gentlemen's total of 201, and then took 10 wickets for 81 runs.

34 Photograph of W.G. Grace taken on the roof of the old Pavilion. In 1895 he became the first batsman to score 1,000 runs in May.

35 & 36 W.G. Grace in action. These photographs may have been taken at the old Crystal Palace ground – Grace is wearing his London County cap.

37 The Eton and Harrow Match, 1895, luncheon interval. The smartly-dressed families and friends of the boys at Eton and Harrow flock to the headquarters of M.C.C. and every seat is occupied. The scene is liveliest during the luncheon interval when the crowds gather on the grass and those "who have been puzzling out the game which they imperfectly understand are free to enjoy themselves. No cricket match throughout the season is more keenly contested than the annual fixture." In 1895, the match was drawn, though greatly in favour of Eton. Harrow, chasing 218 in their second innings to win the match, were 75 for 9 when it ended. This photograph shows the first Grand Stand and the covered enclosures which ran around the north side of the Ground from the Pavilion to the Nursery End.

38 "The Lookers On". An engraving of spectators at the Eton and Harrow cricket match.

39 Gentlemen v. Players at Lord's. The Gentlemen, seen here, are: (back row) Mordecai Sherwin (umpire), W.H. Bradley, A.C. Maclaren, C.L. Townsend, William (W.A.J.) West (umpire); (seated) G. Macgregor, K.S. Ranjitsinhji, W.G. Grace, R.H. Poore; (on ground) F.S. Jackson, C.B. Fry, D.L.A. Jephson. (J.R. Mason was absent.) The Gentlemen defeated the Players by an innings and 54 runs. 1899.

40 Untitled sketch at Lord's, *c.*1900.

41 The M.C.C. team to Australia, 1903-04. This English team under the captaincy of Pelham Warner regained the Ashes with a 3-2 series win. (back row) Herbert Strudwick, Len Braund, J.A. Murdoch, Assistant Secretary, M.C.C. (manager), Albert Knight, Edward Arnold, Arthur Fielder, Wilfred Rhodes, Reginald Foster, Albert Relf, John Tyldesley; (front row) Tom Hayward, Bernard Bosanquet, Pelham Warner, George Hirst, Arthur Lilley.

42 Oxford v. Cambridge, July 1904. The crowds enjoy a stroll on the outfield in the luncheon interval during the University Match.

43 Eton v. Harrow, July 1907. The match continues despite the rain. By this time, pitches generally, and Lord's in particular, were greatly improved by spreading marl or liquid manure, leading to matches characterised by high scores. M.C. Bird, the Harrow captain, scored a hundred in each innings.

44 Servicemen offer loud support at a Baseball Match at Lord's between American and Canadian troops, 28th July 1917, with 10,000 spectators.

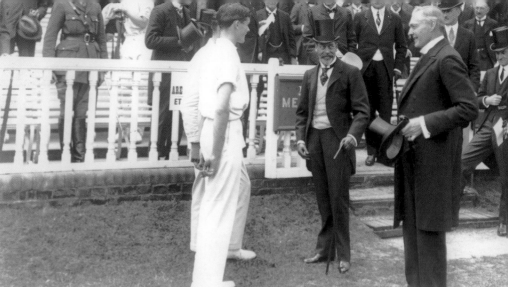

45 The Royal visit on 23rd June 1914, during the Ground's first centenary year. On the second day of the match between M.C.C. South African XI and The Rest, the two captains, C.B. Fry and J.W.H.T. Douglas, are being presented by Lord Hawke, President of M.C.C. to His Majesty King George V. The Prince of Wales (later King Edward VIII) and the Duke of York (later King George VI) are also present.

46 H.M. King George V meets the captains of Eton (C.H. Gibson) and Harrow (W.A.R. Collins) at Lord's on 11th July 1919. This was the first match at Lord's between the schools since 1914. With them is Lord Forster, President of M.C.C.

47 Long shadows frame this photograph of the Grace Gates, first opened in July 1922. The inscription on the gates reads:

> TO THE MEMORY OF
> WILLIAM GILBERT GRACE
> THE GREAT CRICKETER
> 1848-1915
> THESE GATES WERE ERECTED
> BY THE M.C.C.
> AND OTHER FRIENDS AND ADMIRERS

Members were invited to contribute to the cost of the "W.G. Grace Memorial Gateway" as it was then described.

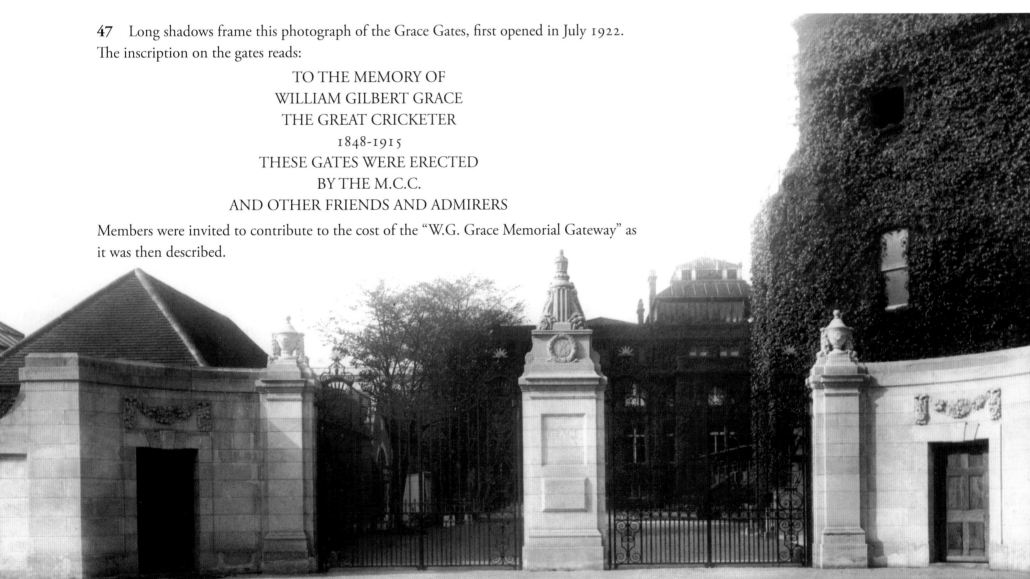

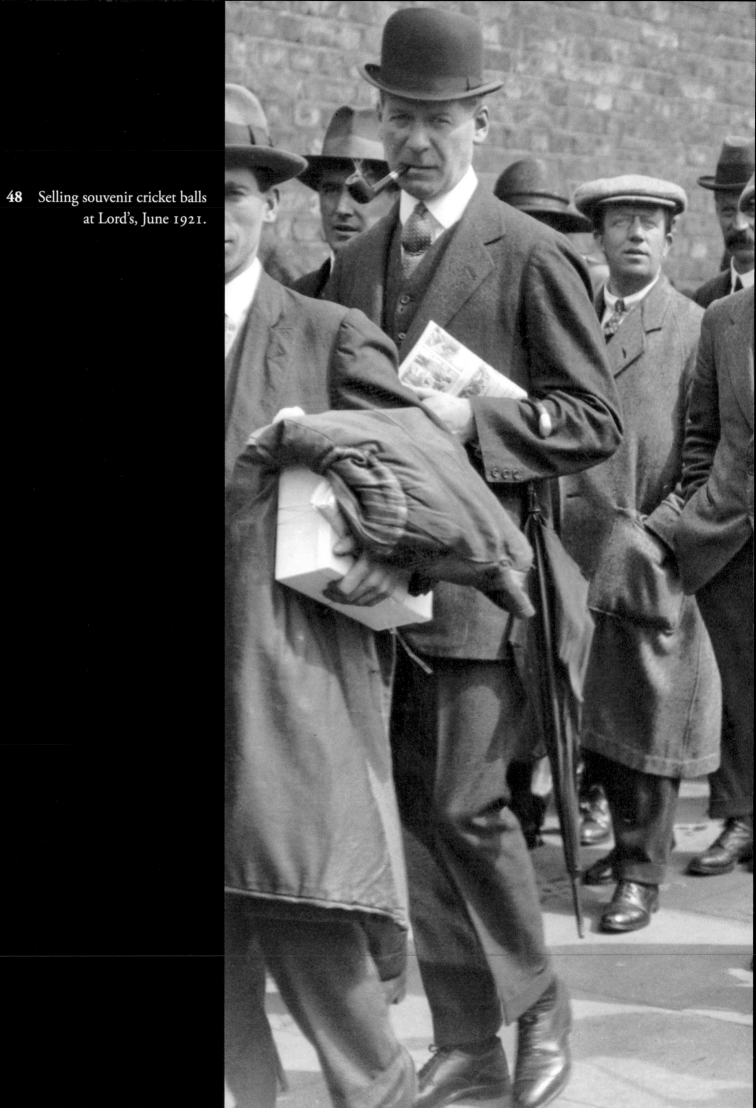

48 Selling souvenir cricket balls
at Lord's, June 1921.

CRICKET-BALL
SOUVENIR
OF THE
AUSTRALIAN
CRICKET TEAM.

49 Eton v. Harrow. Part of the large crowd waiting to enter the Ground, *c.*1924.

50   Spectators pass the time with a game of cards whilst queueing overnight behind Lord's Tavern in St John's Wood Road on the morning of Saturday, 28th June 1924.

51   Some Eton and Harrow schoolboys walking along St John's Wood Road towards the Grace Gates for the cricket match between the two schools, 13th July 1928.

52 A general view of the Grace Gates, the old Tavern Stand and, beyond, the old Tavern, just before start of play in the Australia Test, 27th June 1930.

53 The R101 Airship emerges from low cloud over Lord's on the first day of the Australia Test, 27th June 1930.

54 The Australian team is presented to His Majesty King George V during the Australia Test on 30th June 1930. The King is shaking hands with Stan McCabe watched by the Australian captain, Bill Woodfull (right). Australia won by seven wickets and went on to a 2-1 series win.

55 Australia's Bert Oldfield, the
diminutive wicket-keeper, taking a cine
film of the English team coming out
onto the field during the Australia Test,
28th June 1930.

56 "The Packed Field of the Future." An Australian artist's cartoon published in the
Adelaide News with the caption: "The British Secretary for War (Lord Hailsham) is the new
President of the M.C.C., so the body-line bowling War takes on a more serious aspect".
The 1st Viscount Hailsham was President from May 1933.

57 Don Bradman leaving the nets after a practice knock in preparation for the Second Test Match at Lord's on 22nd June 1934. Widely acknowledged as the greatest Test batsman of all time, "The Don" had a Test batting average of 99.94.

58 "Different Worlds." A woman alights from a taxi arriving for the Eton v. Harrow cricket match at Lord's. She is wearing a full-length organdie dress with cap-sleeved matching jacket, a large drop-brimmed hat and elbow-length net gloves. In contrast to her are two news-vendors whose papers report an attack on women and a launch struck by lightning, 12th July 1935.

59   Elegantly attired spectators approach the Grace Gates for the Eton v. Harrow match at Lord's, 12th July 1935.

60 A schoolboy arrives at Lord's with his sister for the annual two-day match between Eton and Harrow, 9th July 1937.

61 The scene at Lord's during the Australia Test of 1938, painted by Charles Cundall. From the left can be seen the Mound Stand, the Tavern, Tavern Extension, Luncheon Rooms, "Q" Stand, the Pavilion (completed in 1890), "A" Enclosure and the Grand Stand of 1926, with Father Time on high.

62 Wartime at Lord's: benches stored in the Long Room in the Pavilion. The Club's collections of paintings, books, artefacts and memorabilia were taken to the safety of a country vicarage. Lord's suffered modest damage from enemy action. An incendiary bomb landed on the Pavilion roof in 1940, and Father Time was felled by a balloon cable. Lord's, in fact, stayed open for cricket, *c.*1940.

63 Crowds, many of whom had waited all night, queueing for the First Test, Monday, 24th June 1946. This was the first post-war Test Match.

64   Members watching from the Long Room, 1946.

65 Counting the scorecard money in the Printing Office under the Grand Stand, 1946.

66 Huge crowds wait patiently for admission at 1s. 6d. to the Ground in 1946.

67 "No Play Today."
In spite of heavy rain,
crowds turned up
at the Main Gate in
St John's Wood Road,
near the current
position of the
Bicentenary Gates,
hoping that there
might be some play
between Middlesex
and Lancashire,
29th May 1948. (37)

68   Field Marshal Viscount Montgomery being greeted by Sir Pelham Warner at Lord's for the "Victory Test Match" between England and Australia, 1945. This must be a rare picture as Montgomery seldom visited Lord's, but it is said that, when he did, "he liked to make his presence felt".

69 & 70   'The Middlesex Twins'. W.J. (Bill) Edrich and D.C.S. (Denis) Compton stride out to bat, 1947.

Denis Compton, having been offered a professional chance by Pelhan Warner, arrived at the beginning of the 1932 season to be registered as a "fourth-class boy" at 30s. per week for 16 weeks. His work each day from 8 a.m. included pulling the giant roller with 11 other lads, sweeping, cleaning, odd jobs and errands. He also assisted with the Grand Stand score-box and scorecard selling.

  After coaching in the Lord's nets by George Fenner and Archie Fowler, his progress was meteoric. On 13th September 1932 he made 114 opening for London Elementary Schools v. C.F. Tufnell's XI. He made his first-class debut for Middlesex against Sussex in 1936, and the following year his Test debut, against New Zealand at the Oval. In the first Test in 1938 at Trent Bridge, W.J. Edrich made his debut. The careers of the "Middlesex Twins", both ground-staff boys, were under way.

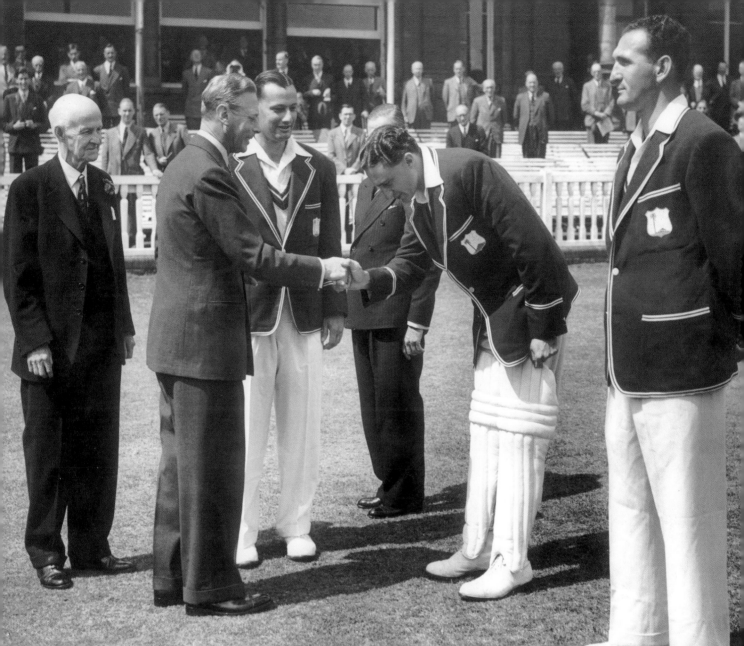

71   H.M. King George VI at Lord's for the Second Test Match against the West Indies, 24th June 1950. The visiting captain, J.D. Goddard, presents J.B. Stollmeyer to the King, and G.E. Gomez is next in line. On the left of the picture is Sir Pelham Warner, President of M.C.C.

72   Her Majesty The Queen visits Lord's, where Middlesex are playing the Australians, 20th July 1953 (not long after the Coronation). The Queen is shaking hands with G. Hole of the Australian team, introduced by A.L. Hassett, the Australian captain. On the left is Mr G. Davies, the Australian team manager.

73 The Dinner, "80 not out", on 24th November 1953 to celebrate Sir Pelham Warner's 80th birthday on 2nd October.

74 Birthday cake for Sir Pelham Warner, with the chef putting finishing touches to the decoration.

75 The Tavern. A new sign is unveiled by the Duke of Beaufort, President of M.C.C., Mr J.G. Dunbar, M.C.C. Assistant Secretary, and Mr R.T. Gaby, June 1953.

76 Aerial view of Lord's Cricket Ground in Coronation Year, 1953.

77 A general view of the parade behind "A" Enclosure on the second day of the Eton v. Harrow match, 9th July 1955. Spectators could watch the match from Coach Mound in the comfort of their coaches.

78 One of two scarecrows, this one in cricket boots and pads, placed in the middle of the turf to protect newly sown grass from invading pigeons. Every year when the seed is sown the pigeons get fat on this expensive seed, so in September 1955 the groundstaff resorted to more drastic methods. This photograph is taken in front of "A" Enclosure, soon to be demolished to make way for the new Warner Stand.

Equally serious was the problem, 20 years earlier, when Lord's, after two hot summers and a mild winter, became the breeding ground for the leather-jacket, the larva of the crane-fly, or daddy-long-legs. The larvae munched their way through the grass roots of Lord's sacred turf. No remedies really worked, and each morning the groundstaff had to sweep dead grubs from the grass.

79   In the Easter holidays M.C.C. organised coaching instruction for schoolboys. Here, H.P.H. Sharp (Middlesex) is giving slip-fielding practice, 6th April 1956.

80   C. Oakes (Sussex), O.W. Herman (Hampshire) and G.D. Morton (Middlesex) are coaching bowling with a group of schoolboys in their Easter holidays, 6th April 1956.

81 The large Saturday crowd watching the third day's play in the Second Test between England and the West Indies, 22nd June 1957. This photograph is taken from the front of the old Mound Stand looking across the Tavern concourse towards the South Clock Tower and "Q" Stand (now the Allen Stand).

82 A very long queue for the Test Match, June 1957.

83 Spectators rush onto the pitch and throng around the players as they leave the field after the third day's play in the Second Test Match against the West Indies, 22nd June 1957. As the scoreboard records, West Indies were bowled out for 261, England winning by an innings and 36 runs. Staff seats can be seen on the roof of the North Clock Tower building, to the right of the second Grand Stand, 1926-96.

84 Aerial view of Lord's, post 1958, showing the
new Warner Stand in the north-west corner.

85   The Tennis Court, started in 1838 and completed in 1839, "at an expense of upwards of £4,000, a proceeding which has tended very considerably to increase the memberhood of the Mary-le-bone Club, seeing that more than 150, amongst whom are the very first nobles of the land, have enrolled their names since the completion of the building." The Club was fortunate to have the champion, George Lambert, as resident tennis master from 1871-85.

86   Henry Johns demonstrating forehand stroke-play off the back wall, 18th June 1959.

87   Henry Johns, appointed to the staff of M.C.C. in 1936, was Head Tennis Professional at Lord's between 1954 and 1975. He coached countless young tennis players, including David Cull, shown here in 1959, who went on to succeed Johns and was Head Professional from 1975 until 2002.

88   England's opening batsmen, R. Subba Row and M.C. Cowdrey, walk out to open the innings in the Second Test Match against South Africa, 23rd June 1960. At the age of 13 Cowdrey became the youngest cricketer ever to appear in a Public Schools' match at Lord's. In the course of a very distinguished cricket career, he went on no fewer than six tours to Australia.

89 The Australians have their first practice at Lord's with captain R. Benaud leading them towards the Nursery Ground, 22nd April 1961.

90 The Australian team in the nets, 22nd April 1961.

91 The sun is shining on a large crowd watching and waiting for the gates to open and admit them to the third day of the Australia Test, 24th June 1961.

92 Spectators enjoying lunch underneath the South Clock Tower boxes on the second day of the Eton v. Harrow match, 7th July 1962.

93 Oxford v. Cambridge at Lord's, 11th July 1962. J.M. Brearley, who scored 113 not out, cuts a ball from D.R. Worsley. Mike Brearley later became one of England's most successful captains, winning Ashes series at home and away.

94 Members of the Pakistan touring team have their first practice at Lord's, 26th April 1962.

95 Members of the M.C.C. touring team attended a Reception at Lord's Tavern on the eve of their departure for Australia. Here the Revd David Sheppard is arriving at Lord's with his seven-year-old niece, Sarah Maxwell, 26th September 1962.

96 Members of the West Indies touring team have their first practice in the nets at Lord's. Garfield Sobers leaps to take a catch during fielding practice, 16th April 1963.

97 The Australian Women's cricket team visit Lord's where they tour the Museum and have some fielding practice. Looking at the Ashes in the Museum are: Marjorie Marvell of Sydney, Coralie Towers of Western Australia, and Helen Lee of Sydney, 13th May 1963.

98 On the opening day of the new season, Freddie Trueman, the Yorkshire and England fast bowler, talks with umpire, Harry Sharp, after being no-balled for the second time during the morning's play between M.C.C. and Yorkshire, 27th April 1963.

99 An Old England XI v. The Lord's Taverners is watched by Sir Robert Menzies, the Australian Prime Minister, 15th June 1963.

100   The England team to play the West Indies practise at Lord's. Team manager and selector, Willie Watson, with a bat gives fielding practice to D.B. Close, F.S. Trueman, D.A. Allen, and F.J. Titmus, 19th June 1963. To the right of the Staff Flats a new house for one of the groundsmen would be built within a year. The Nursery Ground accommodates cricket practice and minor matches.

101   On the first day of the Second Test Match against the West Indies, F.M. Worrell, the West Indies captain, is clean bowled by F.S. Trueman for a "duck", 20th June 1963.

102   G. Duckworth, former Lancashire and England wicket-keeper, scoring during the match, 20th June 1963. In the mid-19th century scorers sat on a perch to avoid being disturbed by spectators. Scorecards were first printed in 1848 on a portable press. Groundstaff boys saw scorecard selling as a source of extra cash. In the 1930s, Denis Compton remembered, "We earned ½d. commission on a scorecard sale, … and took home about £5 a head … in 1934, England against Australia, every boy went home with the giant sum of £14 for the day's work, nearly ten times his weekly wage."

103 Colin Cowdrey, England and Kent, leaves the field holding his arm after being struck by a ball from Wes Hall on the fourth day of the Second Test Match against the West Indies, 24th June 1963.

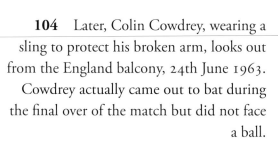

104 Later, Colin Cowdrey, wearing a sling to protect his broken arm, looks out from the England balcony, 24th June 1963. Cowdrey actually came out to bat during the final over of the match but did not face a ball.

105 During the Second Test against the West Indies, a small group break away to watch West Indian cricketers not playing in the match practising in the nets at Lord's, 22nd June 1963.

106 In 1963 about twenty first-class players took part in an M.C.C. experiment, in which wickets were widened by two inches to 11 inches, and the old LBW law was re-instated, providing that the ball must pitch between wicket and wicket. During the experiment, umpired by Frank Lee and Laurie Gray, T.E. Bailey (Essex) plays a defensive stroke to the bowling of D. Shackleton (Hampshire), 11th July 1963.

107 The Australian touring team practise at Lord's. W.M. Lawry and I.R. Redpath collide as they both go for the ball during fielding practice, 20th April 1964.

108 Rain delays the start of the Second Test against Australia at Lord's. Australian players look out from their dressing room: Neil Hawke, Bill Lawry, Grahame Corling and Bobby Simpson, 18th June 1964.

109 Wet weather delays play on the first day, and the wicket is being covered as it starts to rain, 18th June 1964.

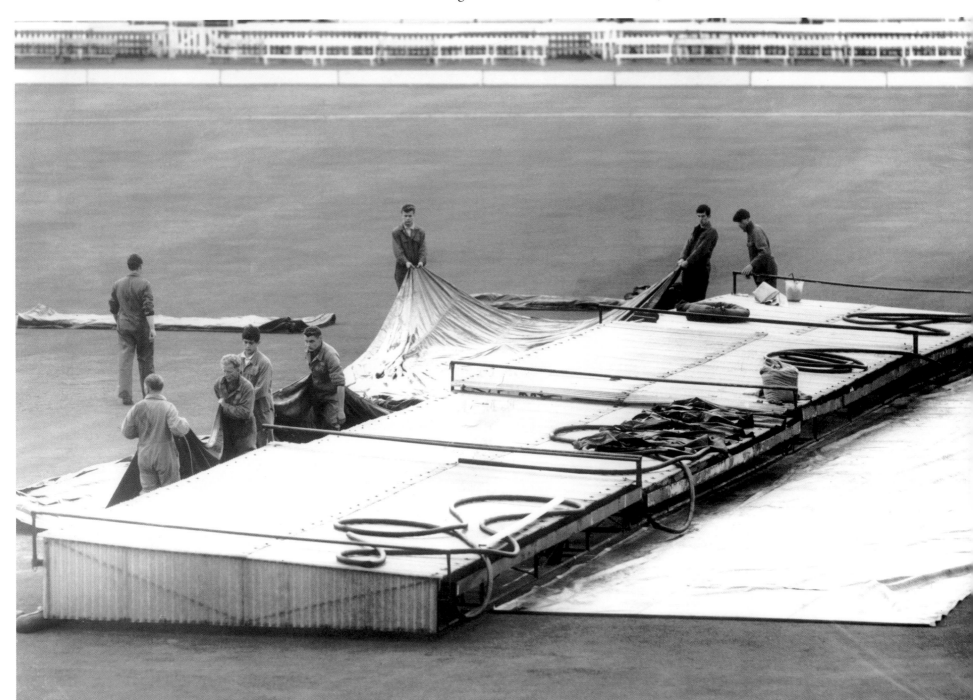

110 Grahame Corling is pictured filming the drying-up operations from the Australians' dressing room, 19th June 1964.

111 The mopping-up operations for the second day: the wringer is in operation on the pitch as groundstaff try to get the playing area ready for play, 19th June 1964.

112   The Australian team inspect the wicket just before play
started on the third day, 20th June 1964.

113   England win the toss and put Australia in to bat. Here
E.R. Dexter tosses the coin watched by R.B. Simpson, the
Australian captain, 20th June 1964.

114   Her Majesty The Queen meets the England team: J.H. Edrich (shaking hands with the Queen), N. Gifford, P.H. Sharpe, and L.J.Coldwell, 22nd June 1964.

115   The day after the shock announcement of his resignation from leadership of the Conservative Party, Sir Alec and Lady Douglas-Home visited Lord's to watch England against South Africa. But rain delayed play, 23rd July 1965.

116   Groundstaff at Lord's trying to clear large pools of water which have collected on the covers and around the wicket area, following heavy rain that has been falling all morning, holding up play in the First Test Match between England and South Africa, 23rd July 1965.

117 Groundstaff had been similarly challenged in June when there was no play before lunch on the fifth day of the Second Test between England and New Zealand, 22nd June 1965.

118 Geoffrey Boycott (England and Yorkshire) ducks under a bouncer from Wes Hall on the second day of the Test Match against the West Indies. The fielder at forward short-leg is Charlie Griffith, 17th June 1966.

119 Her Majesty The Queen at Lord's on the fourth day of the Test Match, when they met members of both teams. Here she is shaking hands with Garfield Sobers, captain of the West Indies touring team, 20th June 1966.

120 An enthusiastic West Indies supporter runs onto the pitch to lift Sobers off his feet to celebrate his completing 100 runs, 20th June 1966.

121 A view of the scoreboard on the fifth day of the Second Test, with the West Indies batting, and Sobers on 163 and Holford, his cousin, with 100, contributing to the score of 364 runs, 21st June 1966.

122 In the same match, a West Indian supporter, wearing a top hat and coloured shirt, and waving a large flag, marches onto the pitch to congratulate David Holford on reaching his century, 21st June 1966.

123 On the fifth day of the Second Test, Sobers looks skywards as a ball from Ken Higgs rolls onto his stumps but fails to dislodge the bails, 21st June 1966.

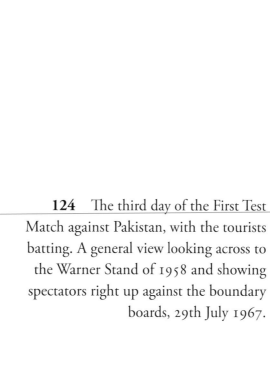

124 The third day of the First Test Match against Pakistan, with the tourists batting. A general view looking across to the Warner Stand of 1958 and showing spectators right up against the boundary boards, 29th July 1967.

125 The Gillette Cup Final between Kent and Somerset. Some Kent supporters parade around Lord's before the match starts, 2nd September 1967. Kent won by 32 runs.

126 A Press Conference in the Long Room at Lord's on the Sunday Entertainments Bill before it came before the House of Commons. In the Chair, and speaking, is Col Michael Ansell (British Show Jumping Association). Others seated are (left to right) Mr N.E. Dixon (chairman of the Auto-cycle Union), Mr A.J.A. Lee (Public Policy Executive of The Royal Automobile Club), Mr S.C. Griffith (Marylebone Cricket Club), Mr A. Hardaker (Football League), Major R. Brooks-Ward (Press Officer, British Horse Society), Mr Shipman (Senior Vice-President of the Football Association), Mr E.M. Miller (Football Association), Mr H. Powell (secretary, Football Association of Wales), Mr E.J. Waltham (Secretary, British Board of Boxing Control), Mr A.A. Gold (Secretary, Amateur Athletic Association and British Amateur Athletic Board). Members of the Press were present, 18th April 1968.

127   Play was stopped on the first afternoon of the 200th match between England and Australia when a sudden freak cloud-burst of rain and hailstones completely flooded the pitch, 20th June 1968. The new Tavern Stand had opened the previous year, with a concourse still present in front of the Taverners' Bar.

128 View of Lord's with the Second Test Match between England and Australia in progress, 21st June 1968.

129 Sunday Cricket. Mr Tony Garrat, Chairman of John Player, and Mr S.C. Griffith, Secretary of M.C.C., sign the contract for the sponsorship of the Sunday Cricket League to be known as the Player's County League after the sponsoring firm, John Player, which was to start in 1969. The total contribution from John Player was not announced, but the counties would be competing for awards totalling £30,000. 9th October 1968.

130 The First Test between England and New Zealand: a New Zealand fielder dives to stop a scoring shot from Derek Underwood, 26th July 1969.

131 Wringers and other equipment for drying the playing area.

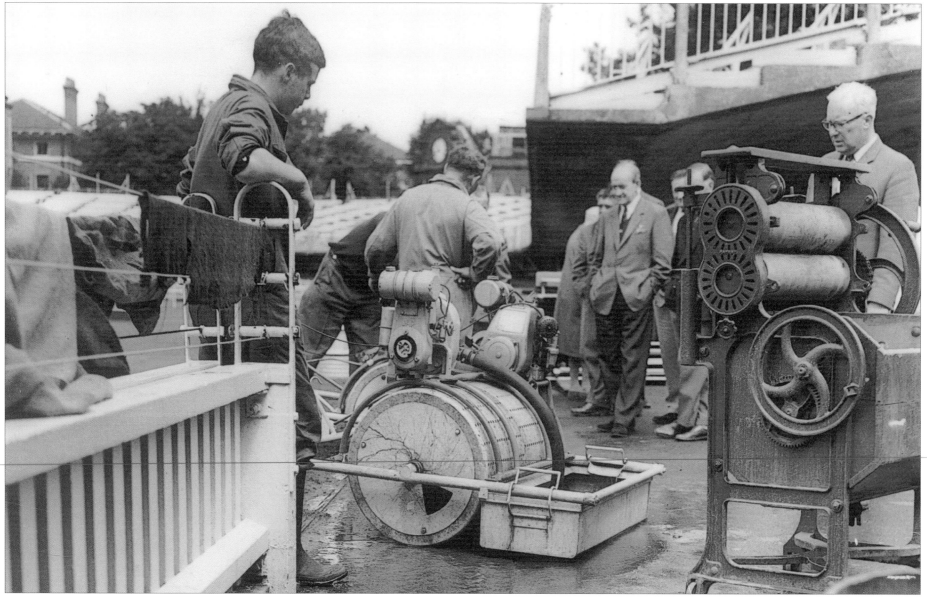

132 Two members of the M.C.C. Works Department remove graffiti painted on the wall in St John's Wood Road by campaigners against the proposed visit to the U.K. of the South African Touring Team. The tour was eventually cancelled by the Cricket Council on 22nd May 1970.

133 The Cricket Council meeting in session to ratify the recommendations of the Test and County Cricket Board concerning the proposed tour by the South African Cricket Team. The final decision on whether the tour would go ahead was to be made later that evening, 12th February 1970. Seated outside the table (reading clockwise) are: Mr C.G. Howard, Mr D.J. Insole, Mr E.H. King, Mr W. Wooler. Mr J.G. Dunbar, Mr A.M. Crawley, Mr G.O. Allen, Mr M.J.C. Allom (Chairman), Mr S.C. Griffith (Secretary, M.C.C.), Mr C.G.A. Paris (Chairman, West County Cricket Board), Mr D.B. Carr, Mr J.A.Bailey, Mr R. Subba Row, Lt-Col. the Lord Nugent, Mr C.H. Palmer. Seated inside the table (reading clockwise) are: Mr J. Norris, Mr B. McArdle, Mr W.L. Jones, Mr A.F. Dawn, Mr T.E. Burrows, and Mr R.A.C. Forrester. Seated by the window, taking minutes, is Marnie White.

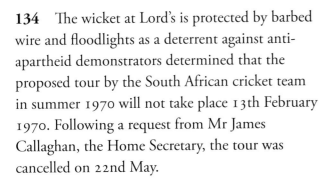

134 The wicket at Lord's is protected by barbed wire and floodlights as a deterrent against anti-apartheid demonstrators determined that the proposed tour by the South African cricket team in summer 1970 will not take place 13th February 1970. Following a request from Mr James Callaghan, the Home Secretary, the tour was cancelled on 22nd May.

135 Mr S.C. Griffith, M.C.C. Secretary in his office, viewing articles in the national newspapers on the cancellation of the South African cricket tour, 23rd May 1970.

136   On the first day of Middlesex's match against Derbyshire,
P.H. Parfitt hammers out a dent in his box with the handle of his
bat, after being hit by a ball from P.E. Russell, 27th June 1970.

137   "Produced by Balfour Films for the Children's Foundation
(Saturday Morning Pictures), a bunch of children and their mad
science master chase across London after a cricket ball gone mad.
They end up at Lord's where the ball is picked up by none other
than Garfield Sobers." Stephen Brassett, an 11-year-old film-making
enthusiast, stands by for action during the making of the film. All
the children are from Islington Drama Club, 23rd September 1970.

PROD. JUNKET 89
DIRECTOR PETER HAMMER   CAMERAMAN TONY IMI
SLATE 2577   TAKE 1
DATE 29-9-70   DAY

138 Jim Fairbrother joined the staff at Lord's in 1968, and was Head Groundsman from 1969 until his death in 1984. The Groundsman of the Year in 1981 and 1982, he had been an assistant groundsman at Trent Bridge between 1953 and his appointment to the staff of M.C.C. Between the Pavilion and the Warner Stand is the Bowlers' Annexe, which originally served as the dressing room for the professional cricketers, who were not allowed in the Pavilion.

139 The Malaysia-Singapore Ligers on a two-week visit to Britain to play M.C.C. and various other clubs take the opportunity to look over the famous ground, 15th July 1971.

140 The England team in the nets in preparation for their match against India, starting the following day. The batsmen in the nets are: Richard Hutton, John Jameson and Ray Illingworth (captain), 21st July 1971.

141 The first day of the First Test Match against India, 22nd July 1971. Here, crowds surround John Snow after he reached his half-century.

142 The following day Sunil Gavaskar is out, caught at slip by Dennis Amiss off John Price for four runs, 23rd July 1971.

143 On the final day Gavaskar, going for a quick single, is sent flying by John Snow as he follows through after bowling, 27th July 1971. This clash made international headlines at the time. Snow later apologised.

144   Don Kenyon and Peter Richardson about to open the batting for Lord's Taverners XII v. Old England XI on 31st July 1971.

145 Almost certainly from the same match, the image itself is something of a mystery. The only record of the match is a scorecard, from which it is possible to suggest that the felled batsman might be Harry Secombe, and the wicketkeeper either Godfrey Evans or Dick Spooner.

146 Spectators crowd the playing area after a bomb scare, 24th August 1973.

147   Fans of the West Indies team celebrate their win over
England at Lord's, 27th August 1973.

148 The M.C.C. team gather at Lord's before their tour of the West Indies, 31st December 1973. (From left): Tony Greig, Bob Willis, Mike Hendrick, Chris Old, Pat Pocock, Geoff Arnold, John Jameson, Derek Underwood, Frank Hayes, Dennis Amiss, Jack Birkinshaw, Keith Fletcher, Bob Taylor, Alan Knott, and Mike Denness (captain).

149 Hockey was played at Lord's into the 1980s. Here, J.L. Neale (Southgate and Essex) scores England's equalising goal against Spain. The final score was Spain 2, England 1, 25th March 1974.

150 A queue forms at the Grace Gates for the Gillette Cup Final on Saturday, 7th September 1974. The day's play was eventually abandoned and the match took place on the following Monday.

151   Supporters of the West Indies during the inaugural World Cup Final against Australia at Lord's, 21st June 1975. A TV cameraman is filming the action (centre). The West Indies beat Australia by 17 runs.

152   Australian fast bowler Jeff Thomson has a cat as a spectator as he practises on the day before the Second Test is to start at Lord's, 30th July 1975. "Thommo" was one of the fastest bowlers ever to play Test cricket, and his partnership with Dennis Lillee became one of the most fearsome in cricket history.

153 The Streaker, Michael Angelow, a 24-year-old seaman on leave, on the fourth day of the match between England and Australia, 4th August 1975.

154 "The Real Maidens". Cricket history was made this day when the England women's cricket team played against their Australian counterparts in a battle for the St Ivel Cream Jug. Here, the Australian team is seen with their mascot on the balcony of the Pavilion as they watch the day's play, 4th August 1976.

155 In the same match, the England team, led by Mrs Rachael Heyhoe Flint, take the field, followed by the opening Australian batsmen, to applause from Members of the Club, 4th August 1976.

156 The original Indoor School, which opened in 1977, was replaced by the New Indoor School, 19th October 1995.

157 Spectators wait patiently for play, delayed for over an hour because of rain, in the one-day Prudential Trophy match between England and the West Indies, 23rd August 1976.

158 Rain, once again, delays the start of a match, this time the semi-final of the Gillette Cup between Middlesex and Somerset, 24th August 1977. So bad was the weather that the match took six days to complete.

159 Two spectators have the Mound Stand to themselves at this quiet start to the first match of the 1978 season, when Mike Brearley, Middlesex skipper, faced the first ball from Mike Hendrick, his fellow winter tourist to Pakistan.

160 David Gower, an England captain with 13 Test centuries to his name, hits a ball for four during play on the second day of the Test against Pakistan, 16th June 1978.

161   Members of the West Indian women's cricket team get in some ball practice at Lord's, in readiness for their matches against the England women's team in the CIS Insurance Trophy (Test Match series) and the CIS Insurance Cup (One-day International series), 1st June 1979.

162   Groundsmen sweeping water off the playing area after heavy rain during England's match against India, 3rd August 1979.

163 The Benson and Hedges Cup Final, between Essex and Northamptonshire, which was due to have been played on Saturday, 19th July, had to be postponed until the following Monday because of heavy rain. Four groundsmen – Neal Wilde, Mick Hunt, Adrian Morgan and Alec Gull – are seen here, sweeping water off the covers.

164 The two umpires, D.J. Constant (left) and H.D. "Dickie" Bird closely inspect the Lord's wicket before their decision on the resumption of play on the third day of the Centenary Test between England and Australia, 30th August 1980.

165 A lone spectator sits under his umbrella as he waits for the rain to stop for the match between Middlesex and Essex, 6 May 1981.

166 Australian fast bowler Dennis Lillee loosens up with the aid of physiotherapist Derek Adler at Lord's when the touring party had their first session in the nets in preparation for the forthcoming Test series against England, 13th May 1981. Dennis Lillee was the outstanding fast bowler of his generation, noted for his fiery temperament, never-say-die attitude, and immense popularity with cricket crowds.

167 Mike Gatting (Middlesex) succeeded Gower as England captain, and scored six Test centuries. He is President of M.C.C. 2013-14. In this photograph, he sweeps Allan Border (Australia) to the boundary. In the next over, Border caught and bowled Gatting for 75 runs, 15th June 1981.

168   On the last day of the Second Test, England declared their second innings at 265 for 8 wickets. Highest scorer was David Gower with 89 runs, and Geoffrey Boycott scored 60. Ian Botham, in his last Test as captain, collected a pair when he was bowled by Bright in the second innings, 7th July 1981. Botham was the supreme all-round cricketer, with over 4,000 Test runs and 357 Test wickets to his credit.

169 A general view of the Ground during the Second Test against Australia, 2nd July 1981.

170 Somerset fans after the Benson and Hedges Cup Final at Lord's,
25th July 1981.

171 View taken from the Pavilion at the
World Cup Final between India and the
West Indies, 25th June 1983.

172 Lord's under a blanket of snow, January 1985.

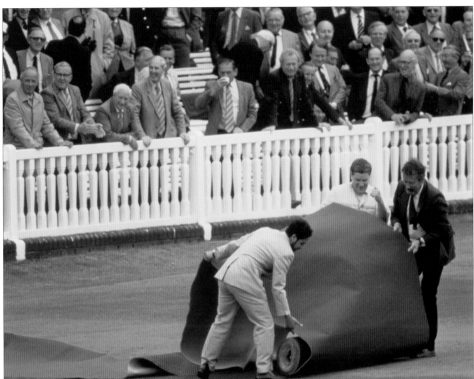

173 Before the Australia Test, the red carpet is rolled out ready for a visit by Her Majesty The Queen, June 1985.

174 M.C.Cowdrey, President, M.C.C., invites bids at the Bicentenary Sale, organised by Christie's, 13th April 1987.

175 H.R.H. The Duke of Edinburgh, on the right, after opening the new Mound Stand, designed by Sir Michael Hopkins. From left to right are: Mick Hunt (Head Groundsman), Lt-Col. John Stephenson (Secretary, M.C.C.), David Male (Chairman, Estates), Sir Anthony Tuke (Chairman, Finance), Hubert Doggart (Treasurer), Sir Colin Cowdrey (President, M.C.C.), 1987.

176 In the Bicentenary Year, the match in August between M.C.C. and Rest of the World was washed out on the fifth day.

177 Denis Compton's forward defensive spade starts the construction of the Compton Stand in 1989. He is watched by John Lelliott (left), Chairman of the construction group, and Lt-Col. J.R. Stephenson, Secretary of M.C.C.

178 Graham Gooch scores 333 for England at Lord's in the First Test Match against India, 1st July 1990. He went on to score 123 runs in the second innings, the aggregate of 456 in a Test match setting a world record.

179   The re-opening of the M.C.C. Museum: (left to right): Dennis Silk, President, M.C.C., Prime Minister John Major and Stephen Green, Curator, 19th May 1993.

181   Clearing snow at Lord's, February 1991. Father Time was relocated when the Grand Stand was replaced in 1996.

180   The Museum's stained glass window. The inscription reads:
THIS WINDOW WAS UNVEILED BY
THE RT HON JOHN MAJOR MP
ON 19TH MAY 1993
TO COMMEMORATE THE
RESTORATION OT THE MUSEUM

182 Catering during the Second Test Match against India, 1st June 1996.

183 E.W. "Jim" Swanton celebrates his 90th birthday with a party in the Long Room, 11th February 1997.

184 Work in progress on the Media Centre, 18th March 1997. It was completed in time for the 1999 Cricket World Cup. Designed by Future Systems and built by Pendennis Shipyard, Cornwall with Centraalstaal from the Netherlands, it was the first all aluminium, semi-monocoque building in the world.

185 Further development of the Media Centre, 2nd April 1997.

186 England captain Graham Gooch is caught by Ian Healy off the bowling of Shane Warne for 29 in the second innings of the Second Test Match between England and Australia at Lord's, 17th June 1993. Australia won by an innings and 62 runs. Warne became one of the greatest bowlers in cricket history, with over 1,000 wickets in international cricket. A five-wicket haul in an innings at Lord's, however, eluded him.

187   The World Cup Final between Australia and Pakistan, 20th June 1999.

188 & 189   Australia lift the trophy after victory by 8 wickets in the World Cup Final over Pakistan at Lord's, 20th June 1999.

190 Graffiti, presumed to be Victorian, on the stonework of the balcony outside the current Members' Bar in the Pavilion. The area was once used as a dressing room and the engraved names of several cricketers who played at Lord's towards the end of the 19th century, including Warwick Armstrong, are visible.

191 Tendulkar is bowled by Hoggard during the First Test Match against India, 28th July 2002. Tendulkar is generally regarded as one of the world's greatest batsmen, second only to Sir Donald Bradman in Test cricket, and to Viv Richards in One Day Internationals.

192 A general view of Lord's in the evening during the Twenty20 Middlesex v Surrey match on 15th July 2004.

193 Her Majesty The Queen greeting members of the West Indies team with captain Brian Lara before the First Test Match, 22nd July 2004.

Brian Lara is one of the finest batsmen to have graced the game. He holds several cricketing records: among them, the highest individual score in first-class cricket (501 not out for Warwickshire against Durham, 1994, the only quintuple hundred in first-class cricket history); and the highest individual score in a Test innings (400 not out against England in Antigua, 2004).

194   Steve Harmison is out lbw to Shane Warne at Lord's, July 2005.
Australia won the Test, but England regained the Ashes.

195 Brian Lara is bowled by Ashley Giles in the First Test Match, 26th July 2004.

196 Brian Lara hooks during the First Test Match, 26th July 2004.

197 Jacques Kallis of South Africa batting during the M.C.C. v International XI at Lord's on 14th June 2005.

198 Andrew Strauss in action against Australia in the Second Test Match, 16th July 2009.

199 Ricky Ponting, Australian Test captain between 2004 and 2011, is considered to be one of the best batsmen of the modern era, along with Sachin Tendulkar of India and Brian Lara of the West Indies. He is Australia's leading run scorer in Test and ODI cricket.

200   During the 2012 Summer Olympic Games, Lord's Cricket Ground hosted the Archery competition in front of the Pavilion. This view was taken during the Men's individual 1/8 Eliminations.

201   The Band of Christ's Hospital School entertains the spectators with a marching display.

202   Usman Khawaja of Australia dives to save a boundary during day three of the Second Investec Test Match between England and Australia at Lord's, 20th July 2013. Prominent are the floodlights above the scoreboard.

203 The Maasai Warriors Cricket Team in action during a charity match at the Last Man Standing Finals at Lord's, 4th September 2013.

f Lord's at the Millennium

hotographer

photography as a child and, after starting his career in international advertising
graphy. Visual documentation of his travels in the late 1990s caught the attention of
ading to commissions in the worlds of sport, corporations, charities and expeditions.
ay continues to balance his work between teaching, commissions and instigating

206 The life of broadcaster, Brian Johnston, commemorated in the
Coronation Garden.

A bat-maker demonstrates his
on a major match day.

s
l
ive

209 The opening ceremony before the start of the 1999 World Cup.

210 Father Time, when the wind is in the right direction, surveys more than Lord's.

211-13 Rain stops play, but never stops lunch. The picnic area and (bottom right) the Food Village are always packed during the luncheon interval. Fans gather in front of the Pavilion (top right) at the end of a match.

214 The puzzling perspective of a woman walking past a poster of Lord's outside the Ground.

215-17 Views of the Tennis Court which, since 1900, has been situated behind the Pavilion. Originally, it was built where the Mound Stand now sits.

218 The Indoor Cricket School used during the 1999 World Cup as the Media Centre. Outside seating for viewing matches on the Nursery Ground.

219 Ball games in the Harris Garden. Before 1932 it was a Lawn Tennis court.

220 Behind the Mound Stand. Like the Pavilion the light roof floats
above the mass of the structure below.

221 Escaping the ground admission charge! Fans find a good vantage point on top of Lord's View in St John's Wood Road.

222 The old public address announcer's box in the Pavilion: it was removed during the building's extensive refurbishment in 2004-05.

223-5   The first floor of the Museum (top) houses the Ashes Urn (bottom left). Turnstiles at the North Gate are checked before the general public can be admitted.

226 The opening match in the World Cup, 1999. Chasing 205, England beat Sri Lanka by eight wickets.

227 Just about
ready – the new Media
Centre in 1999.

228-30 The Nursery Ground (top left) and the Main Ground – 17 acres and barely a mile from the centre of London – make Lord's unique. The television blimp for overhead shots (below) casts its shadow over the outfield.

231 A tour is conducted through the Long Room, prior to the Pavilion's refurbishment in 2004-05.

232-3 A summer's evening at Lord's. After the crowd (top left) leaves much of the playing area is covered for a forthcoming match.

234-9 More Lord's images.

KEEP OFF
THE
GRASS

240 A Member, his head covered by a copy of *The Times*, on the front page of which an article about Shane Warne is promoted.

241 In 1953, London Transport named one of its locomotives "Thomas Lord". After electrification of the railways the name plate was presented to M.C.C. and fixed to the heavy roller which now lives in the Coronation Garden.

Illustration Acknowledgements

Pictures selected from M.C.C. own collection are not specifically acknowledged. Other sources of illustrations are as follows: Getty Images, 27, 33, 34, 37-9, 41-3, 48, 50-6, 58-60, 63, 66, 67, 76, 82, 91, 128, 132, 134, 146-52, 157, 159, 161-5, 168-71, Adrian Murrell/Getty Images, 171, 173, 176; Patrick Eagar/Getty Images, 175, 178, 182, 190-99; David Munden/Getty Images, 186; Mike Hewitt/Getty Images, 187-89; David Klutho/Getty Images, 200; Matt Bright/Getty Images, 201; Ryan Pierse/Getty Images, 202; Christopher Lee/Getty Images, 203; PA Images 46, 47, 57, 71, 73-5, 77-81, 83, 86-90, 92-127, 129, 130, 133, 135-145, 166, 167.